GW00724953

CAPRICORN

THE ARTFUL ASTROLOGER

CAPRICORN

Lee Holloway

Gramercy Books
New York • Avenel

To my children

A Friedman Group Book

Copyright ©1993 by Michael Friedman Publishing Group
All rights reserved.

This 1993 edition is published by Gramercy Books,
distributed by Outlet Book Company, Inc.,
a Random House Company, 40 Engelhard Avenue,
Avenel, New Jersey 07001.

Printed and bound in Singapore

Library of Congress Cataloging–in–Publication Data

Holloway, Lee.
The artful astrologer. Capricorn / by Lee Holloway.
p.   cm.
ISBN 0-517-08259-4
1. Capricorn (Astrology)   I. Title.
BF1727.65.H65   1993
133.5'2—dc20   93-24875
CIP

8 7 6 5 4 3 2 1

CONTENTS

Symbolic rendering of a seventeenth-century astrologer.

INTRODUCTION

Is astrology bunk, or is there something to it? If astrology is utter nonsense, why have so many of the world's finest thinkers, including Johannes Kepler, Copernicus, Isaac Newton, Carl Jung, and Goethe, turned to astrology for information and guidance over the centuries?

Some people may scoff when astrology is mentioned, but even these skeptics are usually inquisitive about their signs. Whenever I attend a dinner party, I ask the host not to mention that I am an astrologer—at least not until dessert—because the conversation invariably turns to astrolo-

In the middle ages, the wealthy consulted astrologers regularly.

gy. When people learn that I am an astrologer, they first try to get me to tell them about their signs and what lies in store for them. Then, in a subtle way, they bring up the next bit of business, which usually concerns a loved one. Finally, as you've probably guessed, they want to know whether the two signs get along.

We humans are an inquisitive lot—we are eager to learn more about our friends, family, lovers, and employers. Astrology is one way to satisfy that natural curiosity.

In the not too distant past, only royalty, heads of state, and the very rich consulted with astrologers; such consultation was a privilege of the elite. Today, astrology is a source of information and fascination for millions; astrological columns can be found in major newspapers and magazines all over the world.

Astrology is not a form of magic. It is a science. Put simply, it is a practical application of astronomy that links the stars and planets with our daily lives. A horoscope is a picture of the stars and planets at a given time, such as that of a person's birth. By examining each planet's position and the relationships of all of the planets to each other at a specific moment, an astrologer can determine your basic personality or predict a general course of events. Perhaps the noted Swiss psychologist Carl Jung summed up the concept of astrology best when he said, "Whatever is born or done at this moment, has the qualities of this moment in time." Astrologers form a continuous link with the past, and each human being, although unique, is part of nature and the universe.

Unfortunately, some people have the misconception that astrology dictates who they are and how their life has to be.

This chart dates back to fourteenth-century Italy. The inside circles represent the element, ruling body part, and orientation of each respective sign.

Medieval illuminated manuscript of biblical characters observing the stars.

Nothing could be further from the truth. Astrology does not remove our free will; it simply points out our basic nature and how we are likely to react in certain circumstances. Astrology indicates strengths and weaknesses, talents and abilities, difficulties and opportunities. It is always up to the individual to use this information, and to live his or her life accordingly, or to disregard it.

Like other sciences, astrology's origins date back thousands of years. There is evidence that primitive peoples recorded the phases of the Moon by carving notches on reindeer bones, and that they may have linked the Moon's movement with the tides, or the snow's melting in spring with the rising of the constellation now known as Aries. As early as 2000 B.C., astrologers were using instruments—carved out of granite or fashioned from brass or copper—to observe and calculate the positions of constellations. These calculations were surprisingly accurate, even by today's standards.

Over time, astrological calculations were refined and the planets were named. The Babylonians were the first to describe the natural zodiac, and their first horoscope dates back to 409 B.C. Centuries ago, people began to examine the stars' potential impact on human emotions, spirit, and intellect. Today, astrology is so deeply embedded in our culture and language that we rarely give it a second thought. The

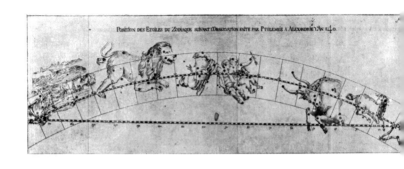

Position des Etoiles du Zodiaque suivant l'Observation faite par Ptolemée a Alexandrie l'An 140.

The twelve zodiacal constellations as drawn according to Ptolemy's descriptions.

days of the week , for example, have their roots in astrology. Sunday is derived from "Sun Day," Monday from "Moon Day," Tuesday from "Tiwe's Day," Wednesday from "Woden's Day," Thursday from "Thor's Day," Friday from "Frigga's Day," and Saturday from "Saturn's Day." Lunacy, which originally referred to so-called full-moon madness, now encompasses all varieties and forms of mental illness.

Before we begin, I'd like to touch upon one final point. Throughout this book, you'll see references to "rulers." A ruler, in astrological terms, has the same meaning as it does in human society; "ruler" refers to the planet that governs or co-governs an astrological sign (see pages 14–15) or to the constellation rising at the birth of a person or event. Everything has a moment of birth: people, places, profes-

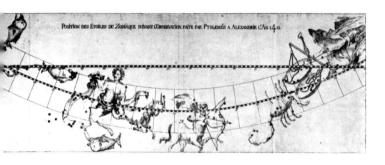

POSITION DES ETOILES DU ZODIAQUE SUIVANT L'OBSERVATION FAITE PAR PTOLEMÉE A ALEXANDRIE L'AN 140.

sions, even ideas; it would take volumes to show you what persons, places, and things your sign rules, but a small sampling has been included here. For example, different parts of the body have rulers, and that body part is often a point of strength and weakness. Gemstones and colors have also been assigned to each sign, although there are varying opinions about the validity of these less important areas. (It should also be noted here that the gemstone assigned to a particular sign does not correspond to the birthstone assigned to that month.) Generally, however, colors and gemstones are said to reflect the specific energy of each sign.

May *The Artful Astrologer* enlighten and entertain you.

Lee Holloway

THE PLANETS

The **SUN** symbolizes the life force that flows through everything. It rules the sign of Leo and represents ego, will, identity, and consciousness.

The **MOON** symbolizes emotions and personality. It rules the sign of Cancer and represents feeling, instinct, habit, childhood, mother, sensitivity, and receptivity.

MERCURY symbolizes the mind and communication. It rules the signs of Gemini and Virgo and represents thought, learning, communication, reason, speech, youth, and perception.

VENUS symbolizes love and attraction. It rules the signs of Taurus and Libra and represents harmony, values, pleasure, comfort, beauty, art, refinement, and balance.

MARS symbolizes action and drive. It rules the sign of Aries and represents energy, the sex drive, initiative, the ability to defend oneself, resilience, and conflict.

JUPITER symbolizes expansion and growth. It rules the sign of Sagittarius and represents higher thought and learning, principles, beliefs, optimism, abundance, idealism, and morals.

SATURN symbolizes universal law and reality. It rules the sign of Capricorn and represents structure, discipline, limitation, restriction, fear, authority figures, father, teachers, and time.

The nine planets that comprise our solar system: Mercury, Venus, Earth, Mars, Saturn, Jupiter, Uranus, Neptune, and Pluto.

URANUS symbolizes individuality and change. It rules the sign of Aquarius and represents intuition, genius, insight, reform, unconventionality, and freedom.

NEPTUNE symbolizes compassion and spirituality. It rules the sign of Pisces and represents the search for the divine, intuition, dreams, illusion, imagination, and confusion.

PLUTO symbolizes transformation and regeneration. It rules the sign of Scorpio and represents power, death and rebirth, the subconscious, elimination, obsession, and purging.

THE ZODIAC SIGNS

J ust as there are twelve months in the year, there are twelve astrological signs in the zodiac. The word "zodiac" comes from the Greek *zoidiakos*, which means "circle of animals" and refers to a band of fixed stars that encircles the earth. The twelve signs are divided into four elements: fire, air, earth, and water. The three signs within an element share many similarities, but each sign in the zodiac is unique. The following section is a brief summary of the qualities of the signs born under each element. (The terms "positive" and "negative" as they are used here describe qualities, and are not judgments.)

The fire signs are Aries, Leo, and Sagittarius. They are termed positive and extroverted. They are warm, creative, outgoing, expressive, idealistic, inspirational, and enthusiastic.

The air signs are Gemini, Libra, and Aquarius. They are termed positive and extroverted. They are social, outgoing, objective, expressive, and intellectual.

The earth signs are Taurus, Virgo, and Capricorn. They are termed negative and introverted. They are practical, conservative, reserved, traditional, and deliberate.

The water signs are Cancer, Scorpio, and Pisces. They are termed negative and introverted. They are sensitive, emotional, imaginative, and intuitive.

The fire signs:

Aries   Leo   Sagittarius

The air signs:

Gemini   Libra   Aquarius

The earth signs:

Taurus   Virgo   Capricorn

The water signs:

Cancer   Scorpio   Pisces

Capri

Symbol: Goat

Planetary ruler: Saturn

Element: Earth

Rules in the body: Knees

Day of the week: Saturday

Gem: Jet

Color: Dark gray

Key words: I utilize

corn

**SOME COUNTRIES
RULED BY CAPRICORN**

Afghanistan
Albania
Bulgaria
Greece
India
Macedonia

The Taj Mahal in Agra, India.

YOUR SUN SIGN PROFILE

No one takes the popular expression "life is serious business" more seriously than a Capricorn. Capricorn is ruled by Saturn, known as the taskmaster, grim reaper, and teacher of the zodiac, so those born under this sign have a strong innate sense of discipline and obligation. Even when Capricorns are young, they seem more responsible and older than their years. But the older they get, the better Capricorns feel, and when they reach their mid-forties, they really hit their stride and appear to stop aging.

Perhaps Capricorns' purposefulness comes from their sense of their inherent longevity. They often feel that adversity is apt to occur sooner

> **FIRST WORDS PROBABLY LEARNED BY A CAPRICORN**
>
> I win!

or later, and they want to be prepared. Part of being prepared means being materially secure, so that's why Capricorn's are usually quite good at saving money. It should be no surprise then that they are also conservative and ambitious, often seeking positions of authority.

Capricorns know that they were born to accomplish much—and that accomplishing their goals takes time, effort, and resolve. Shrewd, hardworking, and intelligent, Capricorns usually achieve their goals. Yes, they tend to be serious, but the legacies of forward-thinking Capricorns throughout history

administrator
architect
bricklayer
builder
chiropractor
contractor
dentist
farmer
government official
industrial engineer
mason
mathematician
mineralogist
mining engineer
musician
osteopath
rancher
scientist
sculptor
teacher

demonstrate the rewards that await them for all their hard work. Imagine a world without the likes of Albert Schweitzer, Louis Pasteur, or Martin Luther King, Jr.

Besides being pragmatic, persistent, patient, perfectionistic, occasionally pessimistic, and ultimately wise beyond belief, Capricorns have a great sense of humor. They love to laugh and to make others laugh, too. There have been many marvelous Capricorn comics. Among them are George Burns (also an outstanding example of Capricorn longevity), Victor Borge, Oliver Hardy, and Danny Kaye, who not only made us laugh, but was also a goodwill ambassador. He traveled great distances to bring joy to the children of the world, demonstrating Capricorn's deep sense of duty.

As you may have guessed, work and the Capricorn spirit are synonymous. In fact, if you are a typical Capricorn, unless you find some outlet for your innate drive and ambition, you will probably be miserable and make everyone else miserable as well. Capricorn occupies the pinnacle of the zodiac, the area that governs career; consequently, Capricorns are born captains of industry and natural leaders.

Success and business know-how is natural to Capricorns; this is reflected in their key words, "I utilize." Although they tend to be shy, fairly cautious, and reserved, they love to teach others what they know, which is why Capricorns make great mentors. Because of Capricorns' propensity for business, many people don't realize that they are creative. But Capricorns can also prosper creatively. (Elvis Presley, David Bowie, Henri Matisse, and Isaac Asimov are just a few examples of Capricorn

Annie Lennox

CAPRICORN DIVAS

Joan Baez
Shirley Bassey
Marianne Faithfull
Crystal Gayle
Marilyn Horne
Janis Joplin
Naomi Judd
Eartha Kitt
Barbara Mandrell
Ethel Merman
Dolly Parton
Sade
Donna Summer

Edgar Allen Poe

creative successes.) Whatever field of work you choose, you are almost certain to succeed, and you generally claim your spoils without a lot of fanfare. Capricorns are much too dignified for that.

As for love and romance, a Capricorn has ample appeal when he or she decides to capture the object of his or her heart's desire. This seemingly cool and aloof sign has a definite attraction all its own. (Mel Gibson and Cary Grant exemplify Capricorn charisma, but in different ways. Mel Gibson's good looks, humor, and wisecracking personality demonstrate the lighter side of the sign, while handsome Cary Grant's charm and elegance emphasized the ability to be winning in a more dignified, refined manner.) Capricorns are very cautious about forming attachments and usually develop relationships slowly. Once you do form a union, however, you are generally deeply committed to making it work.

Mel Gibson's wisecracking nature and earthy good looks exemplify the lighter side of Capricorn charisma.

Romance often takes a back seat to a career, but a Capricorn can make a dedicated partner once he or she decides to settle down. Capricorns will also often take on the problems of loved ones, rather than have them suffer.

Like every astrological sign, Capricorn has positive and negative attributes, and the ability to choose which qualities to express. As a Capricorn, you should know that if you don't act according to your better qualities, others may see you as selfish, cold, materialistic, insensitive, and manipulative. Since Capricorn's rightful place in the universal plan is as one who leads and influences people, individuals born under this sign probably will need to remember that the love and respect of others is as important as personal success. If you keep this in mind, you will better enjoy the great rewards that are your birthright.

COMPATIBILITY WITH THE OTHER SIGNS

In nature, some elements are more compatible and blend more easily than others, like fire and air, and earth and water; the same holds true in astrology. Therefore, some astrological signs naturally interact more harmoniously than others.

The information in this section describes how Capricorn tends to relate to other signs. It provides a guideline to the potential strengths and weaknesses of a relationship between two signs. But remember, these are only guidelines. In the final analysis, the choice is yours.

As an earth sign, Capricorn is most compatible with the other earth signs, Taurus and Virgo. The natural rapport of the earth signs is due to their fundamental intellectual and emotional similarities.

ASTRONOMICAL FACT

Saturn, the planetary ruler of Capricorn, is not only the second-largest planet in the solar system, but also the least dense. This planet would float in an ocean if there were one large enough to hold it. Saturn is the smallest of the planets visible to the naked eye.

Brussels was founded circa 1900.

The water signs Scorpio and Pisces make wonderful partners for Capricorn as well. Although Cancer is also a water sign, it is Capricorn's polar opposite in the zodiac, so the relationship would be a bit more challenging than one with either of the other water signs. In nature, "earth gives water form, and water nourishes earth," and the same is true in astrology. This is the reason earth and water signs are basically compatible.

The fire signs—Aries, Leo, and Sagittarius—are not as compatible with Capricorn as the earth and water signs. Stable, conservative, premeditative Capricorn may find the fire signs' generally impulsive speech and behavior unsettling. Certainly, the fire signs and Capricorn are action-oriented, but they express themselves quite differently.

The air signs—Gemini, Libra, and Aquarius—are also deemed less suitable for Capricorn, because air signs tend to be changeable and highly sociable. Capricorns prefer an agenda, and social engagements, unless they're business-related, aren't their cup of tea.

Martin Luther King, Jr. (Capricorn), and Coretta Scott King (Taurus) are a fine example of a successful Capricorn-Taurus relationship. Martin personified the great strength, determination,

and sense of duty of his sign, as he fought long and hard for civil rights for African-Americans, setting a precedent for other such movements around the world. Hardworking, determined, patient, and deeply loyal (all Taurean qualities), Coretta Scott King was a fine partner for him; she possesses the great Taurean endurance, which enabled her to face adversity and support King's efforts and to continue, along with their two children, to carry on his work today.

TAURUS AND CAPRICORN

Taurus (April 21–May 21) and Capricorn make a good match. Taurus has a warm, easygoing disposition that can give balance to hard-driving, perfectionistic Capricorn. Capricorn, on the other hand, can get Taurus, who is sometimes slow-moving, to put plans into action. Both are practical and traditional, and take a commonsense approach to issues. Since they also share a deep sense of loyalty and commitment, they will work hard to maintain their relationship. This is a highly compatible combination that not only can stand the test of time but also will enhance both partners' lives.

VIRGO AND CAPRICORN

Virgo (August 24–September 22) is another suitable companion for Capricorn, but Virgo needs to be treated carefully because of a tendency to be high-strung and nervous. Capricorn and Virgo share an innate desire for perfection, although the two signs may express this need in very different ways. Virgo is happy to help others and is good at separating the wheat from the chaff. Capricorn can be helpful, but really prefers to manage others. Virgo's quick mind and adaptable nature also complement Capricorn's restless drive and need to succeed. Both tend to be workaholics, so they'll definitely have to work out a master plan for taking turns at handling domestic chores.

CAPRICORNS WHO FOUGHT THEIR WAY TO THE TOP

George Foreman
Joe Frazier
Floyd Patterson

Muhammad Ali

CAPRICORN AND CAPRICORN

Two Capricorns can form a successful relationship, simply because they have such similar natures. These similarities, however, can make it easy for them to fall into a rut, especially because Capricorns are prone to following set routines. This duo would have to work together to avoid this. The potential for power struggles is also common with these two, so it would be wise to clearly define areas of responsibility in the relationship to avoid butting heads. However, their need for

David Bowie possesses the strong will his sign is noted for: he has worked hard to become one of the world's greatest rock and roll stars.

tradition, coupled with a strong sense of loyalty, bodes well for this pairing, provided they try to bring variety into the union.

SCORPIO AND CAPRICORN

 Scorpio (October 23–November 21) has a reputation for being moody and intense, but, like Capricorn, is private and intuitive. A Capricorn-

Dietrich

Scorpio union is one of the most suitable earth-water combinations, because these two share a similar drive and quest for power and influence. Capricorns are more straightforward about what they want than Scorpios, but the intuitional link here will help each partner understand the other's unspoken needs and desires. Both Capricorn and Scorpio possess a certain intensity and sense of commitment that would be a positive influence upon the relationship.

Elvis

FAMOUS CAPRICORNS RECOGNIZED BY A SINGLE NAME

Cézanne
DeLorean
Gurdjieff
Kepler
Kipling
Mao
Matisse
Molière
Onassis
Pasteur
Puccini
Roget
Salinger
Schweitzer
Tolkien

Ethel Merman put her sign's creativity and great drive to work for her—and became one of the top performers of her day.

PISCES AND CAPRICORN

Pisces (February 19–March 20) is a gentle soul who lives in a world of imagination and has a hard time letting go of the past. Capricorn is restless, has both feet on the ground, and is primarily concerned with matters at hand. Thus, Pisces can soothe Capricorn, while Capricorn can help fanciful Pisces deal more effectively with the real world. Pisces also has strong nurturing qualities and loves to help others. Pisces' mild, unintrusive nature can act as ballast for Capricorn's driving energy, while Capricorn can be the force that helps Pisces actualize dreams.

CANCER AND CAPRICORN

Cancer (June 22–July 23) is Capricorn's opposite in the zodiac, and the old saying that opposites attract is certainly true here. Each sign possesses and can offer qualities that the other lacks. Cancer is emotional, while Capricorn is rational. Capricorn is independent and realistic, while Cancer is dependent and can get lost in a world of memories. They both tend to be restless, conservative, and family-oriented, so there may be a certain meeting of the minds in this union. Cancer can also nurture ambitious Capricorn, while Capricorn can help to stabilize Cancer's constant mood swings. There is potential for a happy relationship if both partners are mature enough to accept each other for their differences.

ARIES AND CAPRICORN

 Aries (March 21–April 20) and Capricorn are both go-getters who like to be in charge, but Aries is more combative and expressive. This unusual blend can and does work, but both partners will have to make adjustments all the way down the line. Aries will have to throttle back on impulsive behavior, and Capricorn will have to try to be more flexible. Capricorn can lend stability and determination to Aries' difficulty with follow-through, while Aries can lend Capricorn a healthy dose of optimism, enthusiasm, and energy. A combination of the Capricorn caution and the Aries act-first-and-think-later energies can be dynamic but requires mature partners in order to be successful.

LEO AND CAPRICORN

 A union between Leo (July 24–August 23) and Capricorn has potential, although power struggles are very likely. Like Capricorn, Leo is a born leader, so at least these two will understand this fundamental part of each other's natures. Both signs are also devoted lovers. However, Leos love to lavish the good things in life on themselves and those they love, while Capricorns are always saving for that rainy day that they are sure is just around the corner. And that's the exact source of tension: Leo is expansive, while Capricorn is

A good example of a successful and goal-oriented Capricorn-Leo union is the marriage of George Burns (Capricorn) and Gracie Allen (Leo). For years, these two delighted audiences with their humor and warmth. A typical Leo, Gracie liked being the center of attention and was the perfect foil for George's dry Capricorn wit. They were obviously happily married and the rapport they shared was reflected in their performances. Gracie died in 1964 and George has never remarried. He frequently refers to her in his books and public appearances, underscoring Capricorn's deep commitment to a relationship.

reserved; Leo loves to spend, and Capricorn loves to save. It is precisely for these reasons that this association works better in business relationships than in intimate ones. But if Leo and Capricorn are mature enough to love each other for their differences, they can use the tremendous innate ability for success they each possess to focus their relationship on working toward mutual goals.

SAGITTARIUS AND CAPRICORN

 Sagittarius (November 22–December 21) and Capricorn are an interesting mix. Sagittarians are ruled by Jupiter, the planet of optimism and abundance, and they basically live life in a carefree manner. Capricorns, however, have usually had enough hard knocks in their lives to be more conservative and cautious, thanks to their demanding ruler, Saturn. In many ways, these two are as different as black and white. However, before you dismiss this pairing, remember that people come together for many reasons. If Capricorn has become a stick-in-the-mud, a Sagittarius is just the one to liven things up. If a Sagittarian finds himself or herself overextended or out of his or her depth, a Capricorn could serve as the lifeline to safer shores.

Capricorns are humanitarians, and Kevin Costner's
consistent choice of "good guy" roles exemplifies this trait.

CAPRICORN ACTORS KNOWN FOR THEIR COOL ALLURE

Kirstie Alley
Nicholas Cage
Kevin Costner
Marlene Dietrich
José Ferrer
Ava Gardner
Mel Gibson
Cary Grant
Anthony Hopkins
Diane Keaton
Robert Loggia
Denzel Washington

Faye Dunaway

GEMINI AND CAPRICORN

 Gemini (May 22–June 21) and Capricorn form a challenging combination. Gemini is intellectual, outspoken, and prone to flightiness, while Capricorn is unassuming and down-to-earth, and could easily be injured by Gemini's capriciousness. Gemini is slightly unorthodox, and Capricorn is very traditional. Capricorn needs consistency, but trying to get a Gemini to be constant is like trying to capture a butterfly. This pairing has more differences than similarities, but again there are many reasons why individuals choose each other. Although this won't be a boring relationship, it is not likely to be peaceful.

LIBRA AND CAPRICORN

 A union between Libra (September 23–October 22) and Capricorn is the better of the air sign–Capricorn pairings. Both signs are restless, but partner-oriented Libra may need more from a partner than self-reliant Capricorn can give. For a Libra, life is to be lived as part of a twosome; Libras want to do everything with their loved ones, and they love to socialize. Capricorn may feel constricted by Libra's need for constant companionship. Capricorn is also less

> **CAPRICORN CHOREOGRAPHERS**
>
> Alvin Ailey
> George Balanchine
> Robert Joffrey

comfortable in social settings than Libra, the host of the zodiac, and this could be an irritant in their relationship. There is often an attraction between these two signs, but a union will require compromises if it is to survive over the long term.

AQUARIUS AND CAPRICORN

 Capricorn and Aquarius (January 20–February 18) have in common a co-ruling planet, Saturn. Some Aquarians therefore have conservative qualities that will enable them to interact more favorably with Capricorn. On the whole, however, a Capricorn-Aquarius relationship is not the easiest twosome. Both signs are independent, but Aquarius is the rebel and nonconformist of the zodiac, which could ultimately prove embarrassing to tradition-loving, reserved Capricorn. Capricorn could bring some stability to the changeable life and friendships of Aquarius, but the Aquarian love of change and diversity makes it difficult for this sign to show restraint. If these two do get together, they will definitely make some strange music.

Remember, astrology's compatibility guidelines do not mean that one sign can not have a successful relationship with another. They merely indicate areas where there is potential for harmony and areas that will require patience, adjustment, and acceptance.

Sissy Spacek's preference for playing sincere, no-nonsense roles is evidence of her sign's straightforward and realistic nature.

BIRTHDAYS OF
FAMOUS CAPRICORNS

Diane Sawyer

December 22

Diane Sawyer • Edwin Arlington Robinson • Hector Elizondo

Luca della Robbia • Giacomo Puccini

December 23

Akihito • José Greco • Charles Sainte-Beuve • Susan Lucci

December 24

Howard Hughes • Ava Gardner

Robert Joffrey • St. Ignatius Loyola

Isaac Asimov

December 25

Annie Lennox • Little Richard • Isaac Newton

Cab Calloway • Barbara Mandrell • Sissy Spacek

December 26

Phil Spector • Steve Allen • Mao Zedong

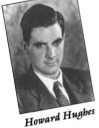

Howard Hughes

December 27

Johannes Kepler • Louis Pasteur

Marlene Dietrich • Oscar Levant • Bernard Lanvin

December 28

Manuel Puig • Maggie Smith

Denzel Washington • Edgar Winter

December 29

Mary Tyler Moore • Viveca Lindfors • Pablo Casals
Marianne Faithfull • William Gaddis

December 30

Michael Nesmith • Davy Jones • Tracey Ullman
Bo Diddley • Rudyard Kipling

December 31

Diane Keaton

Henri Matisse • Ben Kingsley • Diane von Furstenberg
Donna Summer • Anthony Hopkins

Mary Tyler Moore

January 1

J. Edgar Hoover • E. M. Forster • J. D. Salinger

January 2

Isaac Asimov • Julius LaRosa • Roger Miller • Jim Bakker

January 3

Mel Gibson • Victoria Principal • Ray Milland
Robert Loggia • Victor Borge • J. R. R. Tolkien

January 4

Dyan Cannon • Floyd Patterson • Jakob Grimm
Jane Wyman

Robert Duvall

January 5

Raisa Gorbachev • Diane Keaton • Alvin Ailey
Paramanhansa Yogananda • Robert Duvall

January 6

Carl Sandburg • Danny Thomas • Kahlil Gibran • St. Joan of Arc
E. L. Doctorow • John DeLorean

January 7

Nicholas Cage • Vincent Gardenia • Kenny Loggins
William Peter Blatty • Jann Wenner

Nicholas Cage

January 8

Elvis Presley • David Bowie • Shirley Bassey
José Ferrer • Yvette Mimieux

January 9

Joan Baez • Judith Krantz • Fernando Lamas
Crystal Gayle • George Balanchine

January 10

Pat Benatar • Rod Stewart
Jim Croce • George Foreman
Ray Bolger • Sal Mineo

Rod Stewart

January 11

Grant Tinker • David Wolper • Naomi Judd
Rod Taylor • Clarence Clemons
John Molson

Kirstie Alley

January 12

Joe Frazier • Kirstie Alley • John Singer Sargent
Jack London • Luise Rainer

January 13

G. I. Gurdjieff • Jay McInerney • Gwen Verdon • Horatio Alger

January 14

Faye Dunaway • Lawrence Kasdan • Benedict Arnold
Albert Schweitzer

January 15

Martin Luther King, Jr. • Aristotle Onassis • Molière
Gene Krupa • Charo

Benjamin Franklin

Dolly Parton

January 16

Eartha Kitt • Marilyn Horne • André Michelin • Francesco Scavullo
Ethel Merman • Sade

January 17

Benjamin Franklin • Anton Chekhov • James Earl Jones
Muhammad Ali

January 18

Kevin Costner • Cary Grant • Danny Kaye
Oliver Hardy • Peter Mark Roget • A. A. Milne

January 19

Paul Cézanne • Robert Palmer • Jean Stapleton
Edgar Allen Poe • Dolly Parton • Janis Joplin

January 20

George Burns • Patricia Neal • DeForrest Kelly

ABOUT THE AUTHOR

Lee Holloway has been a practicing astrologer with an international clientele for more than fifteen years. The author of a series of comprehensive astrology engagement calendars she has hosted her own television and radio programs including her current show on KABC Talk Radio in Los Angeles. A Sagittarius and the mother of three, she lives in Woodland Hills, California.

PHOTO CREDITS

Grateful acknowledgment is given to authors, publishers, and photographers for permission to reprint material. Every effort has been made to determine copyright owners of photographs and illustrations. In the case of any omissions, the publishers will be pleased to make suitable acknowledgments in future editions.